"Making the decision to truly discover your REAL self is no easy task. It requires honesty, courage, and grace. *Be Free. Be You.* is a testament that real beauty, true inner peace, and an honest perception of oneself happen when we are willing to peel back the layers and understand moments in our life that have brought us to this very moment. Through this book, Achaea teaches us how to be both brave and bold with our inner self. Its transparency personifies the reason we need more REALNESS in today's society."

—CANDACE READ,
stylist at Wardrobe Therapy,
style influence, and fashion blogger

"Redd takes you on a powerful journey to believe in yourself, find the gifts in the struggle, and discover how to authentically and freely be YOU."

—SIMI BIOTIC,
health coach and author
of *Letting Go of Leo*

BE
FREE.
BE
YOU.

BE
FREE.
BE
YOU.

ACHEA
REDD

MINNEAPOLIS

ISBN 13: 978-1-63489-228-5
Library of Congress Catalog Number: 2019938498

Printed in the United States of America
First Printing: 2019

23   22   21   20   19   5   4   3   2   1

Cover design by Luke Bird

Wise Ink Creative Publishing
807 Broadway St NE , Suite 46,
Minneapolis, MN, 55413

To order, visit www.itascabooks.com or call 1-800-
901-3480. Reseller discounts available.

CONTENTS

DEDICATION
9

INTRODUCTION
13

Chapter One
FACING YOUR STRUGGLE
25

Chapter Two
STRUGGLE FORWARD
48

Chapter Three
MAKING THINGS RIGHT
61

Chapter Four
FORGIVING OTHERS IS LOVING
YOURSELF
74

Chapter Five
YOU'VE BEEN BRANDED
93

Chapter Six
CONFRONT REJECTION HEAD ON
112

Chapter Seven
FINDING LOVE AFTER REJECTION
122

Chapter Eight
FINDING YOUR TRIBE
130

Chapter Nine
PUTTING IT ALL TOGETHER
144

Chapter Ten
PAYING IT FORWARD
153

ABOUT THE AUTHOR
164

DEDICATION

This book is dedicated to my late grand-mother, Shirley Ruth Jackson. She was truly one of a kind, not only beautiful but also charming, wise, and outspoken. She was taken from us way too soon. I'm positive that, if she were here today, she would fully endorse the writing of this book. Even though she showed some aspects of a fearless, authentic, rescuing, trailblazing woman, there was also a part of her that was afraid to embrace her true identity because of what others would think or because of societal norms. So this book speaks in the language and cadence of the unspoken whispers in her heart. Here's to you, Grandma . . .

I also dedicate this book to my wonderful mother, who raised me and supported me through every season and phase and never forced a title or role on me. She supported me even through the writing of this book, which was somewhat uncomfortable for her in the beginning because some of the content highlights the flaws in our relationship. Even through that, she has been unselfish and given me wings. I truly believe that she has and always will love me unconditionally. Mom, you are the treasure of my heart and my inspiration forever.

Last, but certainly not least, this book is dedicated to my amazingly patient and handsome husband. You truly are my knight in shining armor. You came in and rescued me from myself in so many ways. You are what I always wanted and didn't know I needed.

I'm sure that being married to a textbook introvert, natural-born rebel, and recovering perfectionist is not easy. I have my issues, but you have loved me through it all, even when it was difficult. You showed me what a God-fearing man looks like and forever changed my idea of what it means to be married and part of a team. You have endured every change, no matter how abrupt, from the tattoos to the nose piercing and haircuts. I love you more than there are words, my love. God broke the mold when He made you.

Michael and Ardyn, you are simply the best kids a mom could have. I absolutely adore being your mama. Thank you for allowing me to be so public about my "farts" (a.k.a. my flaws). It's not easy having a mom known as "the fart girl," but every day you both amaze me with your courage, unconditional love, and acceptance. I hope to give you all that you need from me in this lifetime. I simply don't think I could love anyone more than the two of you.

To Abba, my Divine and Heavenly Father—you are my air and my everything.

Thank you for leading me in every moment, even when I felt the most despair I could ever feel. Thank you for holding me up in those moments in my room when I couldn't stop crying. Thank you for being my absolute best friend and teaching me that you made me perfectly the way I am. I will forever love and trust you as the King of my heart.

INTRODUCTION

Walking into the Bradley Center, I could feel the excitement. The fans, the blare of the bass-heavy music, the smell of popcorn, and the bright lights of the jumbotron: this was the symphony better known as an NBA pregame. I was here, not just as a fan, but as the fiancée of franchise player Michael Redd. I could feel eyes watching me.

"Who is she?"

"I've never seen her before."

"Who is she dating?"

"She doesn't look familiar. I wonder who she knows?"

Okay, so I didn't audibly hear these questions from the stands, but I heard them in my head. Nervous? Understatement of the century! Today, I got to sit among an elite group: NBA wives, fiancées, long-term girlfriends, and sidechicks. The learning curve was steep for everyone, especially for this small-town Midwestern girl. I didn't know if I was up for the challenge. All of a sudden, I felt inadequate, scared, and incredibly lonely.

What am I doing here? Sure, I love Michael, but am I cut out for this? No, I am absolutely not cut out for this! My heart raced as I politely passed by the other ladies. Louis Vuitton, Hermès, Balenciaga—looking at their purses was like looking at a limited-edition, high-end fashion magazine. They could feed a village with those things! Their shoes: amazing. Their makeup: professional. Their hair: not a strand out of place. Their outfits: Wow! You would think they were headed to New York Fashion Week, not a Sunday afternoon basketball game in Milwaukee.

I smiled sheepishly as I took my seat. They didn't seem too eager to have a new lady in their group. Truth be told, I wasn't too eager to be a part of the group either. *I am completely out of my element,* I thought over and over. *What am I doing here? Who am I kidding? This will never work!* My mind was filled to capacity with negative self-talk, but I just couldn't stop. *Did he really think I could fit in? After all, I'm a schoolteacher and a worship leader—a preacher's kid, for heaven's sake! I have no idea what I'm doing.*

Walking into this game, I realized that this situation, this social pressure urging me to conform, was bigger than me. I could literally feel the weight of the pressure. My need to fit in and be accepted was out of control. There was dissonance in my soul. I had just gone from leading worship on a Sunday morning to flying out to be at an NBA game as the fiancée of the franchise player. These were two very different worlds. On one hand, I kind of appreciated the break from life in the church, because the NBA didn't care who my parents were or what my belief system was. On the other hand, I didn't know who I was or what I liked and disliked.

I'd bounced around from one identity to another—first a pastor's daughter, then a singer, and now an NBA player's fiancée. Each one of those identities came with a role that I had to play in order to survive. From what I could tell, these women were perfectly comfortable in their roles. Many of them defined themselves by the designer labels they wore and what season their handbags were from. Many of the engagement rings were gigantic and worn as a symbol of their worth. That wasn't who I wanted to become. I wasn't okay with that role or with equating my value to the things I owned. But at the time, I didn't know my value either.

I wanted with everything in me to make Michael proud. I wanted his colleagues and their significant others to think highly of me. I wanted them to take one look at me and realize just why he picked me when he could've had anyone he wanted. I wanted to show that I was special and unique and that I deserved him. *Who am I kidding?* I thought.

I don't even think I'm that pretty. I hate my natural curls, I hate my body shape, and here I am trying to make everybody else see what he saw when I don't even see it myself. I'm trying to validate a claim that I don't believe. I'm a fraud! I'm a nervous wreck trying to find my way in this world. I want to free myself from the pressure, but I don't know how, and I'm afraid to ask for help. After all, who can I trust? Who would understand? Most everyone I know would just tell me to fake it until I make so I don't mess up.

So I did what I knew how to do quite well; I decided to push my feelings down and carry on. We all know that this never works, right? Pushing your feelings down is like holding a basketball over a gush of water. As long as your hands are on it and the water pressure is low, the ball will stay where you want it. But the second the pressure increases, you no longer have control. It will win over our strength every time because we are human and we have a limit. I tried to hold everything in, but the pressure eventually became too much. I had to decide: either I could keep trying to hold it down, or I could learn how to let it all go. I chose the latter out of sheer desperation.

Since then, I've never felt more awake and alive. This is the time for all us Real Girls. For all of us who are tired of conforming to who we think we should be and are ready to be okay with who we really are—the good, the bad, and the ugly. It's time for us to come alive and awaken to our full potential. It's time to say goodbye to limitations, whether imposed by others or by ourselves. It's time to take the bull by the horns, come out of the dark, unite, and be done with the facade of social media and shallow relationships that lack transparency and depth. Today is the day you take the first step to living your best authentic life.

We live in a fast-paced, want-everything-now society. We feel a need to "keep up with the Joneses." In order to stay relevant, we must do what this gal is doing or what that gal is doing. There is no self-discovery because there's no time for it. Most of us are expected to know what we want to do with our lives before we even graduate high school. We all want the fast track to the American dream. There's a need to have it all right now. The success of one's life is measured in likes, followers, degrees, or money in the bank. The pictures posted on social media feeds have become less about staying in touch with friends or loved ones and more about exploiting others or ourselves, pretending the life we have is amazingly perfect. The pictures are filtered. Every girl who wants to learn basic makeup tips is bombarded with posts of constructed Kim Kardashian look-alikes. It's crazy how much shame is put upon those of us Real Girls out there who just want to throw our kids a basic birthday party but can't escape the "supermoms" out there who have to blast how cool their child's party was. Long gone are the days of a good old-fashioned backyard barbeque birthday party without carnival rides, a pony, and extravagant party favors.

There's beauty in individuality, and that's not showcased enough. When one curated style becomes the measuring stick for beauty, we have a problem. We should never shame anyone for how they look or if they don't subscribe to the trend of the day. There's too much negativity today, plain and simple, and it's trickling over to the youngest generation of women. There's a better way. Our internal and external attributes are important because they're what make us who we are. When we criticize those attributes because of what others think of us instead of accepting ourselves, we lose what makes us unique.

I would like for this book to serve as a guide to help you find yourself. I will take you through the steps I went through to help me attain true happiness, authentic living, and freedom from the opinions of others.

First, it's important for us to go over a few tips and definitions of words that I use in this book before we dive into chapter one. First things first: a Real Girl is any woman who desires to become fully awakened to her potential in and impact on her world. Secondly, for the purposes of this book, the word "fart" is a symbol for mistakes, mess-ups, or things we are not proud of about ourselves. Society would have us believe that women have to meet these standards of beauty and perfection. This leads us to believe that we aren't enough and that we can't afford any internal or external imperfections. My goal was to change the narrative and turn a negative word into a positive one, so I made the word "fart" into an acronym: fearless, authentic, rescuer, trailblazer.

I recently went through a personal challenge in my life that tested my authenticity. Most people, when talking about "keeping it real," are referring to how they conduct themselves or how they behave. I did too. Whenever I talked about being authentic, I was thinking about telling my story and living out loud. And while this is true, it is an incomplete depiction of what this overused phrase means. True authenticity isn't just "doing you"—it's about living what you believe.

My hope is that, after reading this book, you will have awakened your heart and begun the process of self-discovery. True self-discovery takes time but is absolutely necessary to find your happy place. True self-discovery is when you know yourself completely—not only your likes and dislikes but also the *why* behind them. It is when you learn your triggers, the things about you that you absolutely love, and the things that you detest. Sometimes finding our individual happy place includes discoveries we are uncomfortable with, but it's well worth it in the end.

Finding happiness in your life will ultimately give insurmountable peace. I have spoken to several women who have gone through this process, and they all agree that through the good and the bad they still have their peace. I've learned that self-discovery, happiness, and peace are all connected. Self-discovery leads to true happiness. True happiness lends itself to an unshakeable peace. And when you know who you are and are truly happy and full of peace, you will have fulfilling relationships with others and yourself. You will no longer depend on anyone else to be your everything because you will be fulfilled within yourself.

At times throughout this book, I refer to Christian scriptures or other parts of my faith. You have every right to disagree with or not read those sections.

While reading this book, let yourself reflect on both your past and your present. Be willing to go toward places or back to memories you've closed off "for good." Don't rush through the chapters. Reading this book is an individual journey. If you are a notetaker, feel free to jot things in the margins, things that you want to try to model. Highlight points or quotes that you want to remember or use as a mantra. If you are reading and you have your own thoughts based on what you've read, write them in a journal. Who knows—you may even be in the beginning stages of writing your own story or book. It's even okay to put the book down and come back to it in a few days. Sometimes you need a little space to reflect on what you've read. It takes time to unlearn patterns and relearn new ones, so be patient with yourself.

Lastly, if you need to cry . . . cry. Crying is sometimes what growth looks like, and that's okay. I promise.

Now, let's get to work.

Chapter 1

FACING YOUR STRUGGLE

It is a trap to presume that God wants to make us perfect specimens of what He can do — God's purpose is to make us one with Himself.

—Oswald Chambers

When I woke up, I felt strange. I wasn't nervous about anything, but as I brushed my teeth I could feel my legs and arms shaking. This was completely unfamiliar to me. The shaking wasn't visible, so I kept getting ready while secretly hoping that I was delusional. The week went on, but it didn't stop. It became such a distraction that I finally mentioned it to my husband, wanting his reassurance that I was fine. He gave it to me, but that didn't help, so I made an appointment with Dr. Google.

Worst. Decision. Ever. Trust me, if you let Google diagnose you, it will tell you that you're dying. My diagnosis ranged from MS to Parkinson's disease. I was scared, but I tried to believe it was in my imagination and move on. Obviously, that didn't work for me. In fact, it got worse. Much worse.

The more I googled, the more I drove myself into a mental tailspin and the more convinced I became that something was seriously wrong with me. The shaking continued for weeks on end, and my muscles began to twitch at random times. What was once noticeable only to me became outwardly noticeable and more concerning. I battled severe insomnia, which I'm sure made things worse. I lost ten pounds in a week because the thought of eating wasn't appealing to me anymore.

I didn't understand what was wrong with me or why it took so much effort to do the things I used to. Everything was so hard. I knew I wasn't functioning at the level I used to. I used to be able to push past my feelings and still perform. But I couldn't do it. It was like the curtain had closed and the show was over, but no one had bothered to tell me in advance. I had officially reached the bottom, which I perceived as the beginning of the end.

During this time, I seriously considered leaving my family because I thought they deserved more and would be better off without me. In my mind, I was incapable of giving them what they needed and deserved. Day after day, I pondered getting in my car, leaving, and never looking back.

One morning, around three o'clock, my eyes popped wide open and I felt complete fear as I hyperventilated and my body twitched. I thought I was dying. I quickly got out of bed, panting, pacing, and trying not to wake my husband. *Should I call an ambulance?* I wondered. *Am I having a heart attack?* I managed to calm myself enough to go to my basement, and I began to pray. It helped for a little while, but then another panic attack came like a strong ocean wave. All I could do was say, "Jesus! Jesus help me!"

When the panic subsided and I could see the morning light of the sun, I gathered myself and woke my kids up as normal. I tried to follow our normal routine, but I couldn't get it together. I was crying and shaking and nervous. My husband left the house early to catch a flight, and there I was, trying to look like I was in control when in reality I was falling apart. I had to ask my mom to come over to help me finish getting the children ready for school.

When my mom arrived, she found me lying on the couch, hand over heart, trying to calm myself down. She took my kids to school and insisted I go to the doctor. I was so sick from all the adrenaline I could barely walk, but I knew God was there. He got me to the doctor's office safely. How? I'll never know.

I walked into my doctor's office feeling

humiliated. I had been crying and hadn't slept. I, the woman who always looked like she had it together, was just a shell of myself. I felt so emotionally drained that I had no more energy to fake it. I thought everyone was looking in my direction and knew exactly what was going on. I imagined the nurses behind the desk were judging me. The nurse called me back and took my blood pressure. It was through the roof, and that caused me to worry further.

My doctor and his wife came into the room with the most compassionate looks on their faces. His wife embraced me and I fell apart in her arms. I was both ashamed and worried. After listening to me describe my symptoms, my doctor diagnosed me with generalized anxiety disorder and depression.

Trauma from my past and present combined with worry about the future were like gasoline, and all it took was a spark to set my life ablaze. That was my day of reckoning, where I finally met my issues face to face. "Stuffing" my stuff was no longer an option.

It was my responsibility to look back before I could go forward. As hard as it was, I had to journey into my past in order to identify the moments, the experiences, and the circumstances that had built up to the point of an anxious and depressive breakdown. In those moments of reflection, it was hard not to let shame depress me further. I made the conscious decision that I didn't want to live in this personal hell any longer, and it was time to make some changes.

> I made the conscious decision that I didn't want to live in this personal hell any longer, and it was time to make some changes.

As much as I didn't want to ask for help, I'd come to realize I needed it. The first change I made was to see my therapist on a regular basis, not only in moments of crisis. Second, I agreed to take an antidepressant prescribed by my doctor to help give me the extra serotonin I needed. The consistent therapy didn't seem like a difficult change. I love to talk, so talking about myself for forty-five minutes seemed easy enough. The medication was a different ball game.

I'd been on a few different antidepressants for postpartum and premenstrual issues. In the past they'd always helped me, but the thought of having to take a pill every day forever just seemed unnecessary. I thought, *I'm not that bad off. I just get a little nervous every now and then*, and, *Shouldn't I be trusting in God? This is just my lot in life. I'll be fine.* Those thoughts swarmed my head over and over.

Thank goodness they didn't win. I decided that I had nothing to lose. Worst-case scenario, the antidepressants wouldn't work and I'd be no worse off than when I started. Best-case scenario, I'd respond to the medication and it would help balance my brain. I stopped googling antidepressant side effects on WebMD, marched myself back into my doctor's office, and filled the prescription. Best decision ever.

My third change was to reevaluate my relationships with others and with God. In my relationships with others, I'd acted one of two ways: I was either so needy for a friend that I was an open book to people who didn't deserve that openness, or I would close myself off to others as a reaction to the pain of being let down in those relationships. I never had a balance, only extremes, so I knew evaluating my relationships would be tough for me.

But my relationship with God wouldn't be difficult to evaluate—or so I thought. I was a preacher's kid, so I'd known and believed in God practically my whole life. I went to church every Sunday and attended a Christian school. But going through this struggle made me question everything I was ever taught. How could a God who is so loving and powerful allow me to go through what I experienced without jumping in to save me? The last time I checked, I was a child of God; how could He just let me suffer like that? I'm a mother, and I could never let my children so much as stub their toe without my intervention. So what was God's deal? Didn't He love me?

In order to understand and find answers to these questions, I had to look back to my childhood and differentiate the God of the storybooks from the real God. I had to once and for all break up with religion. After all, if I'm a Real Girl, knowing the real God is only fitting. But that's a lot easier said than done. My life was enmeshed with religion and its activities. Religious traditions were why I did or didn't celebrate certain holidays and why I didn't drink alcohol or get tattoos. Religion defined the person I thought I was. It was how I got my value, and ultimately that perspective was my downfall.

My anxiety started young. I know now that it emerged because I didn't feel secure. My earliest memories are of the tension between my parents. I can remember feeling nervous about what might happen between them. Neither one of my parents was raised by their natural father, and because of that they were very hurt. Therefore, they hurt each other. Things changed very quickly between them. There were most certainly good times, but the turbulent times stand out the most to me.

There were nights I'd go to bed thinking all was right in my world only to be awakened by the sound of screaming and crying coming from my parents' bedroom. I'd overhear conversations about other women, and how my father was so sad that he wished to die. A few days later, things were all good and we were at church smiling, either willingly or not. It made me crazy. I didn't know what to believe. The one thing that was always constant was change. That was tough for me growing up.

My mom always confided in me, and in a way, that damaged me. I learned early that I had to protect and rescue. I knew too much, and I had seen too much. There were days I wished I could unlearn or unhear what I had been privy to. I would play with my Barbies and reenact the arguments between my parents. That was my therapy.

My father was much more composed toward me in those early years. We would go to the park to play, and though I had a good time, I was also worried that I would make my father angry like my mom did. The man who showed up at the playground was very different than the man I heard yelling in the middle of the night, just as the woman I wanted to emulate in every way was different than the woman who seemed so helpless in those moments.

My parents tried hard to make their marriage work. My father's ministry was thriving, and his image was all the more elevated by the beautiful family at his side. I felt like my twin brothers were loved while I was put on a pedestal. They were protected while I was expected to be indestructible all on my own. I wasn't allowed to fall apart. I had to be strong for my mom, perfect for my dad, and an example for my brothers. I resented it all.

These issues stayed in my heart through the years, particularly because I felt my father was especially hard on me. By this time, he was pastor at a thriving church, and that was a complicated experience for me. On one hand, I loved to worship. I loved God and I loved to spend time in His presence. On the other hand, I was held to a higher standard because I was the pastor's daughter. Ministry was all I knew, and because of my good behavior, others saw me as the golden child of a budding empire. What those people didn't realize was that I couldn't be like other children, and that was no choice of mine. I wasn't able to play outside after a service or just be silly. I felt awkward most days. I was trained to be a good example for the other children. I was quiet much of the time because I wasn't sure if what I would do or say would be an embarrassment. Other times, I learned good behavior by "crossing the line," and that did a number on my spirit. I learned to shut down and follow a script. My script was church and religion.

When I was alone, I liked to sing at the top of my lungs. Singing was my secret superpower and creative outlet. I never wanted anybody to know I could sing. It was my connection to God. I didn't even know that I was good. At a young age, I wasn't sure where my voice could take me, but I hoped it would take me to New York. I wanted to study acting at Juilliard. One summer day when I thought no one was around, I sang my little heart out. My father came into the room, and then my singing was no longer hidden. I was soon being prepared to share my gift even though I didn't want to. My desire would take a back seat to my responsibilities as a pastor's kid.

The first song I sang in front of the church was by Tramaine Hawkins. I would love to say that I did an amazing job, but my voice cracked miserably and many people laughed at me, including my father. It was the most awful feeling, and worse, no one consoled me afterward. This was my introduction to Miss Perfection. I felt that I could never make a mistake again, or at least never get caught. I couldn't stand the feeling of it. I hated the sound of four hundred people laughing at my expense. It set the stage for a lifelong struggle with being cruel to myself.

At that time, I didn't think of my singing experience as an isolated incident. I figured that there was something very wrong with me. My inner gremlins only added more pain to situations where others criticized me. One Easter Sunday, when I was eleven years old,

I proudly wore a big, pink ruffle dress with ruffle socks. I thought I looked pretty, but a boy I liked hurled an insensitive comment that landed right on my heart. "You look nice," he said, "but that girl over there, she's cold." He was my childhood sweetheart, so it hurt all the more, and again pointed me to the path of constantly judging myself.

By the time I reached my teen years, I cared a great deal about what I looked like. What people said about me carried weight—usually due to the color of my hair and skin. I had to learn how to stick up for myself because no one else ever would, especially the other girls in my class (who would eventually lead me to have difficulties with female relationships later in life). I was not the type of girl who could just let things roll off my back. I felt everything deeply. So when people told me that I had a pancake booty and I looked like a board, I believed it. I got a gym membership to squat my way to a better booty. I bought padded underwear to make my butt look bigger. I tried it all because I believed that if I had a bigger butt and did a million crunches, I would be *perfect*.

Every time I didn't measure up or someone didn't approve, I would use the fact that I could sing or that I was a pastor's daughter to give me an edge over the *competition*. The only real attention anyone ever paid to me was when I looked really pretty or sang a beautiful rendition of a song. So, by default, my appearance and singing ability were what I used to feel good about myself. That was my value, and if the people who judged me on those things were good, God-fearing people, then they must have been right. So I listened and learned. I became an obedient, nonconfrontational shell of myself to appease everyone else.

> I tried it all because I believed that if I had a bigger butt and did a million crunches, I would be perfect.

I didn't want to embarrass my parents or jeopardize their ministry, so I figured out how to be who I needed to be in the moment. But my peers expected me to be someone different, so I learned how to be a hypocrite. I learned to say one thing and do another. I lost my virginity at the age of fourteen because I wanted the acceptance and street credibility. I wanted to experience what all my so-called friends were experiencing. It seemed like a logical choice to make because I was making it all on my own, and the truth behind it wouldn't hit me until much later. In the meantime, I had learned the art of secrecy and was able to go on being who I thought everyone wanted me to be. In my struggle to be perfect, I only learned how to lie to myself and to others.

Action Activity 1

Fearlessly think about your life, both past and present. What are your sources of pain? What's stopping you from living your best life right now with regard to what you've gone through or your current situation?

Share an instance when you questioned your value. #*GetRealJournalOp*

TWENTYSOMETHING

I attended college with the idea that it was just a stepping stone toward ministry. I sang and led rehearsals and I loved it. But something was missing. I was focused on being the perfect this or the perfect that, and I was exhausted from trying to find my own way. I figured that, in order to discover who I was,

I also needed to know who I wasn't. I took advantage of opportunities to step out of my normal world. But the consequences were more than I could handle, and this only agitated my anxiety.

My first anxiety attack was attached to my attempt to protect not just my image but also the images of those around me. I turned twenty-one on a Bible study night, and afterward my boyfriend and I decided to go out to eat. He encouraged me to get a drink. My first thought was, *No, absolutely not,* but that thought was quickly followed by, *Why not?* I felt free, like I was mastering my world as a young woman. As I drank, I opened up to this man and told him personal information about myself and my family.

I learned soon after that he was not as loyal as I had hoped. He told everyone my family business, including private things about my mom and dad. When I found out, I collapsed on the floor and cried in a fetal position, suffering through an anxiety attack.

I thought he was my friend. I was drawn to him because he was so different. He seemed not to care that I was the pastor's daughter, but his intentions were off-track. After that, I felt as though I couldn't trust anyone or talk to anyone about what it was like to be me.

One might think that I immediately broke up with that young man, but I didn't. I was upset, but equally relieved that some of the painful experiences I'd held in had exploded beyond my grasp. After all, many of them were not mine to begin with. I was at a place where I believed every relationship would be something I needed to endure. I had seen that firsthand in my parents' relationship. I was so close

People around me could see that the relationship controlled me in unhealthy ways, but the thought of my own isolation post-breakup was more painful.

to my own pain that I couldn't see how the relationship was breaking me down. People around me could see that the relationship controlled me in unhealthy ways, but the thought of my own isolation post-breakup was more painful.

I'm a firm believer that things don't happen by chance, and I'm a firm believer in God. I believe that God allowed me to come to this point so I could admit that I indeed had issues. I believe He loves us so much that He lets us come face-to-face with ourselves. I had to face the truth: I had not been living but only existing. That existence was hard to keep up because the survival tactics I used in my youth could not stand up to the challenges that life presented to me in adulthood. I was cracking under the pressure, and the moment I admitted it was the moment that my journey to freedom began.

Fear can either inhibit you or motivate you, but it is imperative that *you* decide fear's place and impact in your life. We are born already on a default path that is based on DNA, circumstances, and environment. If nothing changes, we will most likely gravitate toward whatever our default might be. Now, that doesn't make the default bad; it just means that you didn't choose it—it chose you. There is an ongoing war in our hearts between our default and our destiny. There are many battles that involve your purpose. Destiny requires a pursuit. It requires honesty. It requires walking (and sometimes crawling) through the default and fear to get to the other side. But that other side is a freedom like you've never known. It's that wind-in-your-hair refreshing kind of life, the kind of journey so unique that everyone will know that only God could have written it.

Sounds amazing, right? I thought so too. Well, beauties, the first step to that kind of life is recognizing that you're not living it today. Now, if you are, I salute you. But many of you are not, and I want to give you the gentle nudge to lean into the process of releasing every ounce of fear and self-imposed limitation so that you can be free to be you. I'm sure you've heard the expression that honesty is the best policy. This rings even truer when it comes to being honest with yourself. In order to live your best life, you must take the first step of fearlessly facing the things that have caused you pain. That process will look different for everyone. What worked for me may not work for you. What is universal is the desire to change and the persistence to carry it through.

Chapter 2

STRUGGLE
FORWARD

"**S**truggling forward" is not a phrase we hear often. The notion of struggling is usually perceived as negative, like we are being held back or fighting just to keep our heads above water. Struggling forward, on the other hand, is continuing to move forward and resisting the urge to remain stagnant. Could God have given me a miracle and healed me of anxiety in an instant? Absolutely, but He chose to walk with me through the tunnel of my pain so I could understand it. He wanted to deal with the things that I thought too insignificant to reveal to others. He wanted to show me the deep places of my heart and mind.

At first, I saw my diagnosis of anxiety and depression as a weakness. I thought that I, of all people, shouldn't have this problem. I'd grown up in church all my life, and these types of topics are taboo when you are a Christian—and an African American Christian at that. We just don't talk about anxiety and depression as being real illnesses. People would pray over me and say, "God, give her peace." They meant well but didn't have a clue what I was going through. Think about it: when someone is a diabetic and has insulin issues, do we pray over them and ask God to help them be able to eat this bread? No, we don't. They take medicine to help their body process certain foods and avoid other foods altogether. Mental health issues are the same. There's a chemical imbalance in the brain. In my case, my brain doesn't produce enough serotonin or dopamine. Telling an anxious person to calm down or not to worry is like telling a diabetic to just eat the bread. It is a simplistic response to a complex problem.

With anxiety, the body physically doesn't know how to respond to stress. I'm sure you all have heard of fight-or-flight responses before. My brain and body responded to my life like a fight-or-flight scenario, released too much adrenaline, and made me feel completely drained afterward. There are times that I just wake up and feel pretty lousy. Those moments are becoming fewer, but they still happen.

I stood at a fork in the road. I had a choice to make. I could keep holding onto the way I had dealt with life, or I could let go and allow God to reset me completely, even though it would be a process. A reset takes you back to your starting point. I had to identify my starting point and become aware of when the issues came into my life. I knew it wouldn't be easy, but the alternative was a life of continued pain.

Action Activity 2

What are some moments of reality that you have been overlooking or ignoring? *#GetRealJournalOp*

Be anxious for nothing, but in everything by
prayer and supplication, with thanksgiving, let
your requests be made known to God; and the
peace of God, which surpasses all understanding,
will guard your hearts and minds
through Christ Jesus.

—Philippians 4:6–7

This is a scripture that I knew and loved but didn't yet know how to live. I struggled with my family life. My brain was imbalanced. I wanted to be completely accepted by everyone and hated by no one. I had so many things to deal with. I had a choice to make. I could stay where I was, frozen in my pain, or

I could push past the pain and struggle forward.

Neglecting or ignoring the truth of where you are does a disservice to you. It is unwise to go through life with the idea that "this is just the way I am." I want you to challenge your idea of who and where you are and dive into discovering who Abba knows you are and where you're meant to be. It's not an easy journey, but it's worth taking. Why? Because your best self is on the other side of fear.

The struggle is real. It always has been. But struggling is not failing. In our culture, to struggle is to be weak, and nobody wants to be perceived that way. Many women are afraid of being dismissed, so they won't admit their weaknesses, their flaws, or the roots of their deepest pain. Dishonesty robs us of the opportunity to heal. Many of us choose our reputation over authenticity. This is unfortunate, especially since Jesus gave up His reputation to set us free from such bondage.

How do we accept His love and gospel and choose a path of selective freedom?

In John 10:10, Jesus says, "I have come that you might have life and have it more abundantly." It is my view that Abba desires us to be fully liberated, so He often allows a struggle or two, or fifty. Now, that may not *seem* loving, but struggles give us perspective.

One of my dear friends shared with me a powerful observation about her office building that shed light on our journey. The building was surrounded by trees, and she often enjoyed looking out of her window to observe all the birds who made their home in the trees. Her view got even better after some of the trees were trimmed by a tree-trimming company, but then she noticed that birds were flying into her window at full speed and badly hurting or killing themselves. She discovered that the very same branches that were removed had actually been giving the birds perspective. Without those branches in place, the reflective windows gave them a sense that there was the depth of a forest. Those lovely animals were flying into her windows, not knowing that it was an illusion. Those trees, although an obstruction to her, were a blessing to those birds.

There are some seasons when you come up against obstacles and struggles left and right. You sit and wish away the hardships or, like me, suppress them. Sometimes, we're wishing away the very thing that God wants us to utilize to get us to a place of surrender. Do we have some external evil force that may stand in our way sometimes? Sure we do. But more often than not, these struggles are God-approved ways of keeping you from hitting a wall at full force. Those branches are giving you perspective, my friend. The struggles He allows are His love protecting us beyond our understanding.

Struggles are a part of life, whether we like them or not. We all have to face them in some way or another. I don't like them any more than the rest of the world, but I've learned that they have an unbelievable way of shaping our lives and helping us become the "better" version of ourselves that we aspire to become. From the little hiccups to the ultra-mega-colossal problems, they help us grow.

There was a time in my early twenties when I was lonely because I wanted to fit in with my peer group. I didn't have a true sense of belonging. I remember spending lots of time in my room on weekends crying and waiting for my phone to ring with an invitation to do something. The invitations never came, but I learned how to be by myself and like it. It taught me a lot about myself and what I wanted in a friendship. It also taught me to appreciate when friendships presented themselves. Through the struggle of loneliness, I learned to like myself.

If we can somehow learn to recognize our relationship to our problems, we'll be more receptive to the process they take us through. Problems are not merely roadblocks; they're opportunities to learn. Many of us think we would be happier if only this or if only that. But the fact of the matter is that we wouldn't. As humans, we strive for growth, the process of becoming and evolving. Show me a person who is happy being stagnant and I'll show you someone who isn't truly alive or is lying about their happiness. I'm not proposing we go looking for trouble, hoping to run into problems along the way. Rather, when they come—and they will come—accept them. Say to yourself, "Yes, this sucks, but I'm gonna learn from it. Somehow and someday, I'll grow." Know that God knows our end from our beginning, and though He doesn't *cause* trouble, He does allow it. Because He knows that out of trouble He gets the best us possible. Life is full of ups and downs, but it behooves us to go with those flows. Embrace life and all its contradictions: the joy and the sorrow, the pain and the pleasure, the success and the failure, and so on. If we learn to do this and change our perspective, life will become more enjoyable, and we will live more content lives. As I recently heard someone say, "Life will be more of a dance and less of a battle." Practice the philosophy of acceptance. Dance the dance of life without reservation. Going through the struggle will fill you up like nothing else can, and it is only when you are full that you can pour your fulfillment into the world. There is power in recognizing your season and knowing that even the hardships are working together for your good and for God's glory.

#GetRealJournalOp

What Are You Thinking?

One of the ways we struggle forward is by divorcing ourselves from the perceptions of others. Most of how we view ourselves is due to how others see us. We then take those views as our own, and they affect our mental health either negatively or positively. We are not born with low self-esteem. I'm a firm believer that, at the end of the day, God's opinion of us is the only thing that matters. Once we acknowledge that there is a Divine Father Who has given us a purpose from the very moment of conception, other people's thoughts and views of us become irrelevant.

When I was in seventh grade, I had a run-in with a boy. This boy was cruel. He would just look at me, call me ugly, and laugh in my face. Even though he was the only one calling me ugly, I had a hard time not believing him. Why is that? Why do we believe the bad more readily than good? I've always been better at making other people's negative perceptions of me my belief system than at incorporating their positive perceptions of me or my own thoughts about myself. Our perceptions of what others think of us can make or break us and actually deter us from living our best lives.

One of the first things I noticed when I received my diagnosis was how much stigma is associated with mental health challenges. I am a part of both Christian and African American communities, and I experienced stigmas on both sides. But I made the choice to change the narrative. That meant I would have to put myself out there regardless of the backlash. Depression and anxiety can be debilitating, but they are viewed as a choice instead of something a person doesn't have control over. I've had to really educate and facilitate conversations within the community surrounding these topics. This has become something much bigger than me that affects the generations to come, and having this mindset has helped me focus on the solution rather than the stigma. If I would have let those perceptions decide whether

I would come out about my struggles with anxiety and depression, I wouldn't be writing this book. In our quest to find and walk in freedom, we can't be held hostage to our own perceptions or the perceptions of others.

Action Activity 3

List out your struggles and negative beliefs. Then return to your list, and for every negative write a positive. When you are finished, list out ways you can work on embracing the positives and negatives. *#GetRealJournalOp*

Chapter 3

MAKING THINGS RIGHT

Much like the change of seasons from winter to spring, summer, and autumn, so goes life. I have found the metaphor of seasons to be helpful. In my process of obtaining emotional freedom, I spent a great deal of time recognizing where I was emotionally, spiritually, and physically. This was an important step in the journey to wholeness because the season you're in determines your focus. My winter was a time in which I discovered the reality of my life. It was lonely and barren. It felt cold and uncomfortable. I could clearly see the things that had caused me turmoil. They were buried beneath my expectations and assumptions.

I was hopeful that my next season would bring new life. What wasn't apparent was that the spring's new life requires a little heat. It's the heat from the sun that reveals what's underneath. When you press toward freedom, you feel emotional heat and energy. This heat will not to harm you but will instead reveal the things that are standing in the way or lying below the surface of your emotions. You may know of the problems based on your experiences, but do you know the root of those problems? Do you know the things you are responsible for? And if you do, are you willing to make them right?

The mention of making things right can sometimes put people on guard. I get that. But the process of reconciliation is an essential component of freedom, so let's get ready to stretch. When my children bicker, which seems to be pretty frequently these days, they often start the conversation by telling me very quickly about what their sibling did to them. However, I've learned that there are multiple sides to every story. I almost always ask, "But what did you do? How did you affect the situation? Did you bring it on your-self? What part did you play?" Of course my questions are often met with blank stares, fol-lowed quickly by "but she" or "but he." But without that infor-mation, I may imme-diately set in motion an unfair correction or lesson. I need the whole picture in order to assess it fairly, and when I do, I often find that mistakes were made on both sides.

We have to take responsibility for our contributions to our own lives.

We should ask ourselves these same types of questions. We have to take responsibility for our contributions to our own lives, even if our greatest contribution was letting mo-ments pass or not sticking up for ourselves. For some of us, our greatest contribution to our pain is keeping it inside. For some, it is trying to hide our hurt to save face. Some of us may have been messy in the way we deal with others, or perhaps we have accepted dysfunction in our relationships when we were meant to have an extraordinarily loving life. Whatever your truth, own it! Own it with everything in you. It is not until we take full responsibility that the ice begins to melt away from our hearts.

Here's your reality: when you're ready to be free—I mean, truly free—you'll come to a fork in the road. There will be some choices that you must make. You can journey to the place of "whatever it takes" or the place of "it doesn't take all that." In the world of "it doesn't take all that," people hold fast to doing things how they've always done them or the way they've always seen them done. They continue to play the victim (or the aggressor) and believe that the world owes them something for surviving all the chaos they've been through. "It doesn't take all that" is the easy road because you don't have to do anything—but, ultimately, it's a trap to keep you stuck.

How is that possible? How is it that we choose to do nothing? We choose to do nothing for a variety of reasons:

1. We don't recognize our part and believe someone else is to blame.

2. We treat our past as the past and feel no need to return.

3. We don't have the tools or feel empowered enough to initiate the process.

4. We're not ready to tell the truth.

We may not always want to accept it, but transformation requires a sacrifice. My husband is an athlete, and I have seen this first-hand. Michael has a natural talent and an athleticism that are undeniable. But one thing that I have learned from him is that each game requires practice. He did drills, ran miles, lifted weights, and played practice games with the same intensity as the real games. Not only that, but he also studied the game and the players and remained extremely focused in order to be successful. He has taught me that there is a direct correlation between what you do behind the scenes and what you accomplish in the spotlight. So many of us want to publicly portray emotional freedom, but behind the scenes we are bound to the opinions of others and our own self-imposed limitations. We don't want to be stretched as much as we want to be carried.

My adorable son used to experience growing pains. There were times they seemed unbearable for him. As his mother, I didn't want him to be in pain but I also knew that these pains were necessary indicators of his growth. As a mother, I can help soothe the pain, but I can't take it away from him. It's a part of his process. You can't truly be free unless you are willing to go through the hard places, make the hard decisions, and tackle the hard tasks. I like to call those the growing pains of life.

I believe God allowed me to go through a season of growing pains that were particularly intense for me. I spent so much time reflecting on my past, present, and future, and I journaled daily. Sometimes I didn't want to write in my journal or I felt too overwhelmed to write out my thoughts, but I did it anyway. I have a ton of journals that the public will never see, but once I reflected and cleared out all the other "junk," I was able to begin writing my blog, which ultimately turned into this book. When I wrote, events from my past came to mind that contributed to my anxiety. I was responsible for some of these things, and once I accepted that responsibility, the process of healing and restoration could begin.

There were four major events that took place that forced me to take a good look in the mirror. First, I had a cancer scare. That was when I realized that I was terrified of death but also that I also have a tendency to jump to the worst-case scenario before even knowing the facts. Nearly two months later, I found out that I had a kidney stone just lying there dormant, which ultimately taught me I was a control freak and did not like to be caught off guard. If that wasn't enough, because I had worked myself into a tizzy worrying about my kidney stone, I was diagnosed with an eating disorder, anxiety, and depression. On top of all that, my grandmother, with whom I was very close, passed away. That was when I realized I was not in control at all. The thought of not being in control was a tough pill to swallow, but I had to take it.

All these things helped get me to the point of looking in the mirror and humbling myself in order to determine my next moves. Whether they were steps forward or backward, I was determined to have a plan. Yes, it took all that pain to realize I needed to define a direction for my life. The fact of the matter is that I still process my pain. I still get anxious and have depressive setbacks. Some mornings, I have to fight just to get out of bed. There are days when I cry my eyes out trying to understand why my grandmother isn't here and wondering how I'll make it without her. I still humble myself every day in prayer and meditation to ask for help just to get through my day. I've learned that life is a journey, not a marathon. More importantly, I'm learning to be okay with that.

HUMILITY GOES A LONG WAY

Pride is sneaky. My dad often said that pride as an acronym would be "please recognize I deserve exaltation." It took a while, but I came to realize that pride was deeply related to my struggles with anxiety. Pride won't let you admit that you have flaws, struggles, or anxiety. Without that admission, anxiety only grows and becomes more pronounced. Pride and anxiety feed off each other and become a cycle in which you act as though you have it all together when you are far from it. You strive for a perfection that nobody can obtain. This cycle is the very thing that kept me hidden behind my struggles and robbed me of true happiness.

This relationship between anxiety and pride is direct. When we operate in pride, we constantly worry about our anxieties because we think we can control them. That's the root of anxiety: obsession over lack of control. We refuse to acknowledge our anxiety because our pride thinks we can handle it on our own. When we trick ourselves into thinking we have absolute control, we become a slave to our problems or struggles.

A child learning to ride a bike without training wheels is a great visual for this problem. If you've seen this, you know there are really two types of riders. There is the rider who wants the teacher to put their hand on the back of the seat and the rider who wants a completely hands-off experience. The teacher's primary job is to show the rider how to balance without too much reinforcement, but the teacher also knows that falling is likely. That's why the teacher likes to stay close. But if the rider refuses their help, often out of pride, the teacher will pull back, even to the point of watching the rider fall to the ground. News flash, friends: we cannot handle anxiety and fear on our own. We need people around us to help us when we fall.

Coming to a place of humility was refreshing for me. When I released my fears to God, He rushed in to help. I was relieved that He would see me through. During this time, I had to have tough conversations, write hard emails, and make decisions with newfound clarity. It wasn't easy, but I remained humble through it. That place of honesty and vulnerability was so amazing that I still live there to this day. I'll never leave it because I have discovered a powerful truth; when we release our heaviness, we receive the beautiful joy of freedom. Freedom emotionally and spiritually. Our willingness to be vulnerable and honest with ourselves and others produces unshakeable joy and peace in our lives.

With my vulnerability came the magic of restoration. There are many relationships in my life that are stronger, more defined, and more enjoyable because I was willing to step out of pride and into my freedom. You have to be willing to put yourself out there, or you will never know that freedom. Shake the fear and jump in headfirst. You have to trust the process, even though parts of it may be uncomfortable. Telling your story is never meant to embarrass you but to liberate you. What's even more beautiful is the freedom that is passed on to others from your liberation. As we disclose our faults and shortcomings, we find we aren't alone.

Action Activity 4

How can you take responsibility for your reactions and actions? Ask yourself, what role do you play in your struggle? What can you change within yourself? *#GetRealJournalOp*

Chapter 4

FORGIVING OTHERS IS LOVING YOURSELF

Forgiveness sometimes gets a bad rap. Many of us assume that if we forgive those who wrong us, we do it as a favor to that person. Unfortunately, that mindset is the deception. Forgiving others is more for you than for them. Most of the time, the people who have betrayed us have moved on with their lives while we wait for some miraculous and melodramatic thing that will make them see the error of their ways and come back to us. Does that ever happen? Yes, sometimes. But more often than not, it doesn't.

I once heard someone say that unforgiveness is like drinking poison and waiting for the other person to die. I've sat on the side-lines of life far too long waiting for others to realize they were jerks. It got me close to a nervous breakdown and threatened the very existence of my purpose. I'm no longer interested in that life. I made a choice, and although the process wasn't instantaneous, the choice allowed me to live life differently. I'm not perfect, so I must also forgive.

Humility is the gateway for amazing experiences of restoration. As we walk through apologizing, transforming, and aligning our hearts with what and who our Divine Father says we are, we are led to release people through our forgiveness. Please notice that I didn't say to *drop* people. This process of forgiveness is also an act of compassion.

Many of us think we know what compassion is, but truthfully, a lot of us have no clue. I'm included in that bunch, by the way. I started reflecting on 1 Samuel 16:7: "Men and women look at the face; God looks into the heart." Hmmm . . . How many times do I just look at the behavior of a person and never at where it's coming from? A lot. This makes me a really unhappy person sometimes. I'm convinced that focusing on someone's guiltiness makes me feel justified in my anger, bitterness, and unforgiveness. Plain and simple, I feel it gives me the right to be mad. That's the very thing that kept me walking in unforgiveness for so long, and it didn't make me happy.

We need a strong will to move past someone's actions to see the source of their behavior and empathize with them.

Don't get me wrong: we aren't to be doormats and tolerant of malicious and deviant behavior. However, there has to come a time in our lives where we exercise our will and move past our lack of compassion. We must move past our need to be justified and right and into a happier place of contentment and peace in our lives. We need a strong will to move past someone's actions to see the source of their behavior and empathize with them. I often ask myself, "Do you want to be right or do you want to be happy?" Happiness and mental peace win out every time. I believe that if we practice this with people, our lives will be fuller. We will grow as humans, and our relationships will be stronger than ever.

My father and I have had an up-and-down relationship. I remember the not-so-great times more than the good times (and there were plenty of good times). I had always been taught that to get to heaven, you have to forgive. So I would forgive, but I hadn't gone through the process of living out forgiveness until I began to submit to the journey toward emotional freedom.

It was during my fourth year in therapy that I began the process of grieving the loss of the father I always wanted in order to accept the father that I had. Is my dad a good man? Absolutely! But there were things growing up that I needed and didn't get because my father wasn't able to give them. Growing up, I saw myself as a pretty rational child. All I ever needed and wanted was a conversation. I wasn't naturally rebellious; I was naturally curious. There's a difference.

When I was sixteen, I worked an at athletic store in the mall. One evening after my shift, my parents saw me jump on my male coworker's back. We were horseplaying and there was absolutely no romantic interest whatsoever. But my father was overprotective and obsessed with people's perception of me because, in his mind, I was a reflection on him. I was grounded for a very long time, not to mention lectured on how poor my judgment was. I honestly didn't and still don't know what the big deal was. I was very playful back then, so I couldn't understand why he made me feel so ashamed over something so small. That incident filled my heart with rage toward my father. I often felt that I couldn't live up to his standards. This left me feeling powerless with him, and we had years of struggle as we tried to find common ground.

That incident was just one of many that kept me and my father at odds. As far as I knew, we were worlds apart and there was nothing more I could do about it, even with therapy.

When I was able to finally show up and be honest in my truth, I had a conversation with my father that changed our relationship. It was a moment of breakthrough. I felt compassion for him that I had never experienced before. To be honest, I can't really explain where it came from. Maybe I felt so connected to him in that moment because I acknowledged my own struggles with depression and anxiety. I now realize that they run in my bloodline. He did the best he could. It must have been tough for him to be a young husband and father and, on top of that, an up-and-coming preacher in the African American church, which didn't believe in mental illness. There were times he was so sad that death was appealing to him. He wasn't suicidal, but there were times that he just wanted the pain to stop. That was the hand I was dealt because that was the hand he was dealt. I had to step out of my hurt and pain and get a different perspective. I came to a place of empathy. You have to see someone's side with fresh eyes and not hold it against them.

I think one of the most important lessons that I learned during this six-year journey is to give myself space by crying when I need to cry and taking a nap even when I don't think I need one. I'm learning to pat myself on the back and say "good job" when I'm able to have hard, honest conversations, tell someone exactly how I'm feeling, and make no apologies about it. I own what's mine and reject what's not.

For example, I thought I was going to therapy to fix my dad and to learn to better "deal" with him. This all stemmed from a deep desire to be a better mom to my children. I never once thought it was about me. I never once thought that I was this little girl in this grown-up woman's body. Before, I really would take so many things personally. I would own everyone else's mess. I would own everybody else's rejection of me. I would take it on as my own. I would overanalyze and criticize myself. I would pick myself apart because I felt like somebody had something against me. But now, I've learned to just let go of the issues that aren't mine. Letting go makes me happier, lighter, and freer to own up to my part of it because I don't have as much stuff to work through.

How do you discern what's not yours? I can only offer my example. My dad not being who I needed him to be was not my responsibility. His problems weren't my history—only my responses to his problems were. If I fail to own up to my responses, then that's my responsibility. You can't overly obsess about things you can't control; you can only process them. You have to look at the circumstances and say, "Okay, that's yours, and this is mine." Whatever your part, deal with it and move on.

In the early days of therapy, my therapist had me write a letter to both of my parents that I would never send. Once I read the letter, processed it, and ripped it up, I realized I wasn't done. I still wanted to be mad. I wanted a reason to continue to behave in my anger. That was over five years ago, and I'm happy to say I just finished the process of letting it go. It was long and hard because I was simultaneously learning the skills of forgiveness, acceptance, empathy, and compassion. The more I forgave myself, the easier it was to forgive others. I was able to walk in forgiveness because I was able to see the situation from the other person's vantage point. The process of letting go changed my life and enabled me to be the change in my family. It's amazing how interconnected yet separate all our paths are. By changing the narrative in my heart, I brought restoration and hope to my life. I became the change to facilitate change.

My therapist was a huge help. She told me right in the beginning that most of my therapy would happen outside of her office. She asked hard questions that I needed to answer before I could have the conversation with my father. I learned that we have to walk through those hard questions in order to move forward. The problem isn't looking back to move forward; it's staying back. We should always be in a place of discovery, even in recovery. At the end of the day, some people want to stay mad. They want to have an axe to grind and find comfort in being dysfunctional. That dysfunction is familiar and gives them an excuse.

Michael and I are both preacher's kids, but we grew up in very different households. We communicate two very different ways, and I noticed that, no matter what we were communicating about, I was reverting back to this little girl. I had to ask myself, "What is this really about?" "What's the real issue here?" "Why am I feeling like this?" "Why am I self-sabotaging relationships, waiting for the bottom to fall out?" *Why* is the real question. I think that deep down inside, we always know. If nothing else, we know that something is not right.

Although taking the spiritual bypass route of overspiritualizing everything is common and fairly comfortable, it's not the greatest choice. You can give partial control of your problems to God, but you have to do some work on your part as well. I didn't take the spiritual bypass route; I elected to do the work and let God guide what I did. When you do this work, you have to get real honest with yourself and with Him too. You have to ask God and yourself, "Why am I like this? "Why am I having these problems?" "What are the painful moments that shaped me?" If we don't deal with our stuff, it will deal with us.

"It's just the way I am" is often a cop-out for "I refuse to deal with my stuff." People create their whole identities around their shortcomings, and there are enough dysfunctional people in the world to enable them to do that. But owning your shortcomings—that's what it means to be a Real Girl. You have to name them and take responsibility for them. You can't let fear keep you from opening up. You have to be so preoccupied with being free that you don't care about others knowing your flaws. The thought of being free has to be more appealing to you than the thought of whether people will stick around.

I don't know anybody who's gotten to a place of freedom without some stressful or traumatic event happening. Those growing pains present us with opportunities to change or to stay the same, but we don't come out unscathed. Forgiveness lets you turn toward the person you were before you were wounded. It brings you back to the freedom you knew. I'm convinced that in order to experience true freedom in forgiveness, we must go back to a place of innocence. Consider a carefree and joyful child, and then consider what happens to them after a traumatic event. Say they run out into the street and almost get hit by a car. In the future, no matter if a car is present in the road or not, that child will grow up always worrying that one day someone will hit them. They often transfer that fear onto their own children, and so on. They were changed by something that happened to them.

The same is true for you and me. We are changed, often in negative and challenging ways, because of what has happened to us. When we focus on the pain, we will nurse it, curse it, rehearse it, or be limited by it. That is, unless we choose to release it through the process of forgiveness. In order for this child to move on, they must forgive the person who almost hit them.

Empathy is the highest point of forgiveness. It's understanding the context and understanding that those who wronged you (whoever they may be) probably did the best they could with what they had. For the child, they will need to understand that the driver could have been distracted by something out of their control and most likely did everything in their power to keep from hitting the child.

The misconception in the religious community is that forgiveness is instantaneous instead of continual.

Empathy changes your perspective. The misconception in the religious community is that forgiveness is instantaneous instead of continual. I often refer back to the life of Jesus. Whether you believe He was real or a fictional tale, consider this: Jesus must have been burdened during His three years of ministry. He understood His assignment and yet stood in the midst of mistreatment, hate, and being taken for granted by the very people He was serving. We still do it to Him to this day, yet He has never withdrawn His love, grace, and compassion toward us. It is my conclusion that this stance could not be possible without walking in forgiveness—continually. His act of releasing us while He was being crucified has been to our benefit because we have the opportunity to accept His love and to be accepted into the Kingdom of God.

LETTING GO

Freedom to me looks like unapologetically living out loud, being who you are, and blazing a trail—no matter what it costs you. This means we must let go of fear, rejection, bitterness, anger, comparison, jealousy, self-hatred, self-criticism, guilt, the past, and shame. Our culture feeds some of these dysfunctions. I think sometimes we're raised in them. We inherit them a little bit, and our parents perpetuate them. The only way that you can be free of anything is to breathe and let it go. This isn't a simple process. Prayer, meditation, and work of the heart and of the head need to be done.

Letting go and releasing what you've held in can be a difficult journey, but it's necessary in order to get from where you are to where you want to be. A year or two ago, I was in constant pain in my hips. On the surface, though everyone diagnosed me as being overworked as far as my exercise regime, I reminded myself of how I held onto things from my past, from my parents, and from my friends (or people who I thought were my friends). I harbored all of it inside, and it was showing strain on my body.

There were a lot of things that I held against my mother that I hadn't released and that I held because I didn't want her to feel any pain. Even in that, I was being a martyr, self-sacrificing so I wouldn't have to hurt her. That caused me such dissonance.

The hard part about forgiveness is that, so much of the time, we're so full of our own pain that we can't hear or feel anyone else.

And even if we do feel it, it's usually from our perspective, not their perspective, so we don't have an honest view. But when I really tried to become a better communicator, I had to become an active listener, not just with my ears but with my heart. As my mom and dad talked to me, I would close my eyes and just imagine myself as a better communicator, and I began to feel it. That was when the gift of connection came alive in me. For the first time, I was able to experience the beauty of human connection when I could actually feel the other person's heart.

Most of our lessons on prayer should be based on empathy. We often block empathy with sympathy. We are drilled and conditioned to be sympathetic; however, with sympathy you aren't challenged to really see the other person or feel their pain. Empathy is to feel it and respect it. We can do that. Even if it feels awkward, it's worth it. It breaks up the hardness of our hearts. It's freeing to wake up and know that you don't

have anything in your heart against anyone.
You'll add years to your life.

Action Activity 5

Make a list of people who have wronged
you and how. Did you do anything to them
or anyone else that resembled their offense?
Don't make excuses for their actions or yours,
but just as you are able to explain and justi-
fy your actions, try to empathize with them
and see things from their viewpoint.

Once you are ready, make a phone call or
write an email or letter to make things right.
Be willing to be brutally honest, but be polite. Make sure to adjust your expectations;
this is not meant to help you get back in relationship with them, but to set your soul free.
#GetRealJournalOp

Chapter 5

YOU'VE BEEN BRANDED

For most of my life, I was associated with a label—usually one I didn't place on myself. In my youth, I was the pastor's daughter. As a young adult, I was the head of worship and arts. When I married, I was known as an NBA wife. Tack on sister, friend, and mom to that! All I knew were labels. They dictated how I acted, what I wore, where I went, and how I spent my time. Labels come with expectations, most of which are not healthy. I became so caught up in the roles and titles that meeting expectations became more important than the experience of being in those roles. In fact, the process of upholding those expectations inhibited my ability to fill the roles of wife, sister, daughter, friend, and mother. I could feel little tugs on my heart, the inner voice of my soul pushing me to pursue the dreams I once held dear. Expectations had molded me, and I felt that stepping away from roles would mean a loss of ground, a personal defeat, or a poor reflection on those who depended on my faithfulness.

In September of 2016, my life changed. I went with my husband to South Carolina, and we met up with our dear friends Damon and Tammy Thompson, a couple that are like family to us. They are our mentors and accountability partners and have seen us through some really tough times in our marriage, Michael's career-ending injuries, miscarriages—you name it. They are absolutely incredible individuals that we love and have a great deal of respect for.

The plan was to meet up with the Thompsons for lunch to kind of catch up about life and what was new with us. I really thought I was better than when they last saw me. After all, I had been in therapy and had done some work on myself. There had been a lot of issues that therapy uprooted, and I'd had to unlearn a lot. When we got to the restaurant, we greeted each other as we normally would, ordered our food from the deli counter, and grabbed a seat. I thought we were just going to shoot the breeze with them. We started talking; I can't recall exactly what I said, but I had a moment of transparency with them. Damon began to speak to me about things that only I knew. For years I had struggled with eating disorders and body-image issues that stemmed from my childhood and that I'd never felt comfortable addressing publicly. I hadn't even shared these things with my husband. He began to uproot things that only God knew were there.

I cried and cried to the point where I felt almost empty. I felt like sinking under the table and bawling. It was like I had left every part of me on the table. After walking away from that encounter, I felt like I knew nothing. I felt naked. Everything I had known had been done away with. All the things I thought God felt about me and everything I thought I knew about Him were completely gone. I actually had no memory of any of those ideas at that moment. It was a vulnerable and uncomfortable place.

Damon asked me to take a ninety-day break from anything that was in the way of getting to know the real God. He said that getting to know the real God would give birth to the real Achea. When I got back home, I was in a state of shock. I had no idea what had just happened to me. But a month and a half later, I started having panic attacks because this new discovery was the death of the old me and the birth of the new me. My body was trying to hold onto this old me, and the new me emerged through all of it.

It was a very painful process for two months as I put the old me, my old feelings, and my old ideas to rest and let the new me emerge. Since that moment, Numbers 15:38

has been my scripture. I'll never forget it because the moment it came alive for me was the moment I was branded. I never had to worry about what anybody else thought of me or what they would say about it. It didn't matter how I was branded by my clothes or style. It didn't matter if people didn't "buy into" me because, from that moment on, I believed that God's opinion of me was the only one that mattered. Abba, my Divine Father, had branded me with His plan, His purpose, and His desire for me—not just as His servant but as a daughter, friend, and lover. That has resonated with me for the last year, and I have never felt more alive, more awakened. I am more sure of myself, more confident, and more fun to be around since getting to know the real God, because He helped me to discover the real me.

Of course, growing up in the church and being around so many powerful people within the religious community, I had divine encounters with God. In Christianity, particularly the denomination I grew up in, we believed in asking Christ to come into our hearts and giving our lives over to the Lord. I gave my life to the Lord at an early age, but I'd never had an encounter like this one. I'm of the mindset that all the encounters that I've had led me to this one.

There were times when I wanted to quit upholding the expectations of others. The real me wanted to come out and play, but because of the labels and roles, all she could do was stare out the window. Most of my life, my laughter was from my head, not my heart. I wanted to be happy, I really did, but I was imprisoned by the shackles of misidentification.

The mislabeling led me to countless hours of comparison, standing in the mirror pinching whatever fat I could find. I have struggled with the exercise form of bulimia for many years. I was so cruel and hard on myself. When I was happy, I ate. In fact, I overate. When I was sad, I didn't eat and used starvation to punish myself for not being perfect. I remember overeating only to go to my room and do about a thousand crunches until I could hardly laugh. I would weigh myself all day, reducing my value to the number on the scale.

I knew I had a problem, but what could I do? Who could I talk to? After all, eating disorders weren't for black girls, and especially not for preacher's daughters. Besides, of the people I trusted, most thought I was "fat," had a weird shape, was unathletic, and had skinny legs. I was often called "pancake butt" because my rear end was flatter than the average black girl's. If my loved ones thought I wasn't good enough, then I probably wasn't. Right?

It wasn't until Abba reintroduced Himself to me, affirming not only His love for me but also that I was His good work, that my mindset began to change. I had to get to know Him before I got to know me. Isn't it a beautiful thing, that Abba never asks of us a sacrifice that He's not willing to make Himself? He was so jealous for me that He removed from Himself the labels I'd put on Him and took the risk to truly reveal Himself to me so that in turn I would take the labels off myself. It didn't happen overnight, but over time God modeled it for me. He was like, "Daughter, I got you. I've been here from the very beginning. Through all your ups and downs. You have no clue how to be authentic, so let Me show you how through My authenticity." That began the process of authenticity for me. Really finding out who God was and losing myself in that helped show me who I wanted to become and who I was created to be. That experience literally rocked my world.

Don't get me wrong: there are times that, by default, I go back to yesterday in either my words or my actions. Sometimes I attempt to wear the old labels even though they were uncomfortable. Every time that happens, I remind myself that there's more work to do, because I'm seeking the familiar again.

Today, it saddens me to see so many people mislabeled and misidentified based on the expectations that someone else put on them. In the Bible, we have a story of a man who became a king. King David was said to be a man after God's heart. God liked him, not because he was perfect or did everything right but because he was honest and humble. It is often said that God loves everyone, but can we say that He *likes* everyone? I don't think we can. When David was a young man, he volunteered to fight Goliath, a giant standing over eight feet tall. As David was preparing for his fight, Saul—who was the present king and trained in battle—wanted to show David the ropes. He thought that if he let David wear his armor in battle, it would help him win. While to some that may seem like a great idea, because Saul was older and clearly more experienced, David didn't agree and requested to just go in with his normal shepherd's clothing, a slingshot, and stones. Well, as the Bible records it, that worked out pretty well for the youngster. He defeated Goliath and became the hero for his people.

What's the correlation between David and us? Today, we have a lot of Davids wearing Saul's armor to defeat giants, when all they need is a slingshot and a stone. When we put on armor that is not our own, it costs us the battle. We'll spend precious time trying to adjust and risk the chance of getting hurt in the process.

PEARLS AND SPIKES

Anyone who knows me knows I am a loud talker. I am physically incapable of whispering. For years, it was drilled into me that ladies should be seen and not heard. I've been told everything from "you need to dial it back" to "no man wants a loud wife." This concept was foreign to me. I was never trying to act masculine, but I was given a loud voice, perhaps in preparation for my career in public speaking. Growing up, I always looked at my loud voice as too aggressive and as a flaw. My mom was a big proponent of this quiet virtue that I could never master. She meant well, but she was training her daughter the way she was trained. We have to be very careful in rearing future generations. Sometimes, we discount and discourage something that God is going to use. Sometimes,

Sometimes, we discount and discourage something that God is going to use. Sometimes those quirks aren't meant to be worked out.

those quirks aren't meant to be worked out. I'm of the mindset that God thinks in the bigger picture—that's why we need His mind, His eyes, and His heart to think, see, and feel like Him. Lovelies, God wants to use your beauty and your ugliness, your joys and your pain, your weakness and your strength. Though it may seem contradictory to others and trivial to you, nothing with God is a mistake.

A year ago, my husband and I went on a little shopping trip. As we were browsing, I came across some satin shoes with a pattern of alternating designs—pearls and spikes. I chuckled as I picked them up, and knew I had to get them because they were an accurate depiction of who I am. Pearls are delicate, classy, sensitive, refined, and unspokenly feminine. Spikes are edgy, flashy, unrefined, and, if touched the wrong way, *ouchy*. These two couldn't be more opposite from each other. As I made my purchase and walked through the mall, I reflected on that thought. I decided it's good to be a little bit of both. God likes the contrast; in fact, He's the King of contrast. God's very nature is a contrast. Why do you think we have male and female? It's the best of both sides of Abba. God is love, compassion, and beauty. He is also strong, mighty, and too big to be contained. Let Him use your pearls and spikes, no matter how unpopular they are. Let Him brand you with His seal of authenticity. Let Him help you strip the other brands off your identity. Let Him become your identity.

WHO ARE YOU REALLY?

> *But God told Samuel, "Looks aren't everything.*
> *Don't be impressed with his looks and stature.*
> *I've already eliminated him. God judges persons*
> *differently than humans do. Men and women*
> *look at the face; God looks into the heart."*

—1 Samuel 16:7

Samuel was a prophet—someone who could see into the future by divine inspiration—whom God had sent to pick the new king of Israel. However, as he went to the house of Jesse, David's father, he was drawn to one of David's brothers. He was most likely attractive and strong in stature and had all the outward makings of a king. But God instructed His spokesperson to look at one of the other brothers—in this case, the one who was tending the field. You see, David had proved himself to be integral, good-hearted, and humble while shepherding. That is who God wanted, the least likely candidate, the one who was least qualified.

Although this story took place a long time ago, it is similar to the situation of women today, in that we are forced to define ourselves by what's popular or trendy. We are made to focus almost entirely on our outward physical appearance, status, achievements, and accolades to dictate our worth. God looks into the heart, the inner being of a person. The outward appearance can change—rapidly, might I add. These labels ultimately box us in and leave little room for growth beyond them. In addition to their confining nature, labels also divide us and enable us to continue in our unending comparison of ourselves to other women. When we perpetuate this type of behavior, we are unable to become who we were spoken to be from the beginning of time.

Being the significant other of an NBA player is almost like being a member of a secret society. You're in the very small percentage of the population whose husbands got picked out of all the thousands of athletes who were talented enough to play. Basketball Wife 101 goes a bit like this: There are labeled divides between the significant others of the players. You have the girlfriends, you have the fiancées, you have the wives, and you have the sidechicks and groupies. You are treated differently based on your title, and women of the same title are then subdivided by the size of their partner's salary. When Michael and I first started dating, my only saving grace was that he was the franchise player, so I was treated very well. However, people with my label were expected to be together outwardly at all times, without a single hair out of place, and they had better not wear the same outfit, shoes, or purse twice. If you bucked against that system within that community, they would gossip about you. I remember wanting so badly to just wear tennis shoes, jeans, a T-shirt, a baseball cap, and a ponytail, especially when I was pregnant. But because of my lack of identity and my need to be accepted by my new peers, I just surrendered and was miserably uncomfortable. So I paraded in stilettos up until I was thirty-seven weeks pregnant. I hid my feelings easily and no one knew how I felt. I mastered the art of secrecy and living a double life. I was bound to the opinions of others. I was afraid to be me, mostly because I was unsure of who I really was and also because I didn't want people to think I was less beautiful and put together. It was a living hell. And guess what—no one was responsible but *me*! The social requirements did exist, yes, but the people who really mattered, my hubby and God, didn't care as long I was happy and comfortable. I was the one who insisted on keeping up the facade.

As you've read through my struggles, I

bet you've wondered, *How can I break free of labels and be free to be me?* Well, it's not as hard as you may think. The hardest part is just following through. And even though there will be setbacks, you have to keep pushing. The best thing you can do is get to know the Divine Father and get to know yourself. Once you discover those things, you don't compromise them for anyone. There are no labels except the ones the Divine Father gives you. We are works of art in motion. Period. Of course there are certain core things that may never change, but it is in our DNA to evolve no matter who we are or what our belief system is.

Beautiful ones, I've decided to be fearless. I'm done with the opinions of others, whether in the real world or in the fake world that social media has created. My beauty is not predicated on the length of my hair or what the scale says. I don't have to be a part of twenty boards and committees to be of value. I no longer have to earn acceptance. Remember our opening scripture; the only opinion that matters is God's, and I'll take my cue from Him. What He says and thinks, I'll believe, because it's based on the contents of my heart. You are enough, and you are worthy. Yes, that's right, along with every one of your imperfections. So what do you say? Are you ready to forget what others think and focus on the truth of who you really are? Although it's an ongoing journey, it's well worth it.

Action Activity 6

What are some of the labels you've chosen for yourself? What labels do you think others have placed on you? Write out a plan of action for you how you plan to free yourself from those expectations and roles. Be realistic, kind, and gentle with yourself. Rome wasn't built in a day. *#GetRealJournalOp*

Chapter 6

CONFRONT
REJECTION
HEAD ON

*Since this is the kind of life we have chosen, the life
of the Spirit, let us make sure that we do not hold it
as an idea in our heads or a sentiment in our hearts,
but find its implications in every detail of our lives.
That means we will not compare ourselves to each
other as if one of us were better and another worse.
We have far more interesting things to do with our
lives. Each of us is an original.*

—Galatians 5:25–26

Rejection is a painful occurrence. It makes
you feel inadequate and alone. It contin-
ues to speak negativity to you long after the
comment or event. Rejection seems to like to
repeat itself in many different contexts. It will

keep coming after you until you overcome it. The rule of thumb in life is that if you don't deal with your issues, they will deal with you. The difficult thing about rejection is that it is most likely rooted in a deep wound that you received during a time when your defenses were down. For me, the roots of rejection started growing when I was young. There were plenty of experiences I had in school, at church, and even as an adult when I had to put on my big-girl pants and face the reality of these roots.

When I was in first grade, I moved to Heritage Christian School, where I was the only black person in the entire school. Day after day, I was ousted by my peers. I sat by myself every day at lunch and recess. It was a nightmare, and I had to stick it out for the entire year. I can't say that I remember much of anything else from that time. That was when the fear of being rejected started, and when I began to internalize other people's opinions of me. From that moment, I was determined to work to earn people's affection and adoration.

As a child, I remember being terrified of critique. In my mind, there was no such thing as constructive criticism. It was all bad. Most of that came from the lack of trust I had in the people who criticized me. I didn't believe that those people actually had my best interest at heart. Most of the time, there were critiques of what I did wrong but not enough praise for what I did right. For a child whose love language was words of affirmation, that was devastating. I always felt like I should be doing more in order to attain more recognition, but much to my chagrin, that never worked out for me. I was always looking for that "more," even in my adult life.

What happens when you're a kid and you spill something, and your mom and your dad have an overly dramatic reaction? Their severe reaction is probably mostly about the inconvenience of cleaning it up, but that doesn't translate to a child. It translates to

"How could you be so stupid?" or "How could you be so careless?" and this adds fuel to the inner critic. It starts out very, very young.

Another example is when kids start asking questions. They start off unafraid and don't think anything they ask is too silly or far-fetched, but then someone tells them that they ask too many questions or tells them to stop talking. That sends a message instantly.

I've also come to accept that I can't change other people's behaviors. I can only control my response.

The child feels obnoxious or stupid. Before long, they begin to criticize themselves so others don't do it first. That's why for me, it didn't feel so bad when I was the one criticizing myself over others. *I'm not cool,* I thought. *I don't have this. I'm not that.* It felt better that I was saying those things about myself rather than facing judgment from others.

I've learned to accept the fact that I don't like being rejected, and I can't stand someone not liking me. I've also come to accept that I can't change other people's behavior. I can only control my response. I always try to catch my kids doing something right so they never feel there's a bigger emphasis on what they need to work on. Each of us has a little girl inside that felt hurt or rejected at some point. My little Achea rises up from time to time, and I'm learning not to reject her again but to embrace her with open arms.

A few years after my therapy and treatment, I went to a football game with my husband. Because of my anxiety and introversion, this type of social situation made me very nervous. I have a tendency to overthink everything, both what I say and what I don't say. The continual conversation that goes on in my head is unreal. So here I was, at the game with my husband and thinking, *All is well. I've confronted everything. I feel great.* I ran into a young woman who I hadn't seen in quite some time. There was no exchange other than a half smile, and the tension got really thick. This messed with me a little bit, mainly because this woman was a peer and in this particular situation she was the only one I knew considerably well compared to the others who were there. As much as I tried to push my feelings down, ignore how I felt, and pass it off as nothing, the feelings of rejection started to come on even stronger. As I sat there, I started boiling on the inside. I started to have this inner monologue about how I wasn't the cool kid at the table, how I didn't have as much money as them, how I was so glad I was not in high school anymore.

All these scenarios went through my head, giving life to a situation that wasn't really a situation. I was assuming that this young woman was a part of the story in my head, but that was ludicrous, because she didn't know how I felt. What I had to do, instead of ignoring my anxiety, was to put my hand over my heart—as silly as this may sound—and say, *There she goes again. There's the little six-year-old girl on the playground who was forced to play by herself and was rejected by many of her peers.* I had to keep comforting and soothing myself, both the little girl who had been rejected and my adult self in the present moment. When I started to acknowledge that my younger self was in the room and very much a part of me still, I was able to start to confront the rejection.

As I said earlier, one must acknowledge that there is an issue with rejection and deal with it because, until it is dealt with, there will be situations with people that will bring out that child who was rejected or let down. The feelings don't go away just because we ignore them. So once I acknowledged the six-year-old Achea, I was able to move forward. I could say, "Maybe she's tired. Maybe she's getting flustered. Maybe she's getting settled." Once I was able to acknowledge, confront, and handle it, this young woman and I had an amazing conversation and talked the night away. It was pretty cool. I had never handled anything like that before. I didn't realize that I still needed to practice self-care in those situations. I thought I would be completely comfortable with myself and in my skin, and that was not the case.

Deep down, I still have this inner critic. From time to time, it tries to resurface. We all criticize ourselves. It doesn't matter where the critic comes from—whether from overly critical parents, a perfectionist streak, or a fear of failure—we all criticize ourselves. It's important to be aware and not deny the presence of our inner critic. In some ways, the inner critic is good because it allows us to keep working toward our goals and can help us become better people. But at what point is enough enough? If you have a perfectionist streak, a fear of failure, a fear of disappointing people, or an issue with wanting to please everyone, then the inner critic can become dangerous and out of control. You might pick yourself apart until there's nothing left to pick, and even then continue to feel like you are not enough.

I think our Divine Father allows difficult situations to happen so that we can see our position and need for Him. The minute we think that we've arrived, we are smacked in the face with reality. For me, it didn't feel the best at first, but I didn't let that stop me and was able to confront something that was uncomfortable. Conversely, some of us don't like to address issues like this. We prefer to tell ourselves that we have it all together because we're often more comfortable with the illusion of who we are.

Action Activity 7

Make a list of seven things that you absolutely love about yourself. Focus on internal attributes. Each day, spend time reflecting and encouraging yourself with a different attribute. *#GetRealJournalOp*

Chapter 7

FINDING LOVE AFTER REJECTION

We all want to find our knight in shining armor. The person who will be our partner for life. Although I wanted love, I didn't think I deserved it because of all my drama and baggage. On Sunday, August 10, 2003, all of that changed. That morning, life for me began as it always did. I rose early to head out to church. As I arrived, I was met by my adorable friend Joan and we began making small talk. Little did I know, this particular conversation would change my life forever.

She began talking about how a few gentlemen were inquiring about me. They were all athletes, some at Ohio State and some professional. I didn't understand what they wanted with me. I mean, the last several years of my life I had been in what I call a "Christian bubble." I barely went out to anything in the city. I was somewhat hidden. How did they even know who I was? I was a bishop's daughter and a worship leader, for crying out loud; certainly I wouldn't fit into their worlds. We couldn't possibly have anything in common. Right?

My now-hubby's name came up, and I asked, "Does he love God for real?" I just wasn't impressed that easily. I was teaching high school and in a good space regarding relationships, so I didn't want to jeopardize that.

Joan answered, "Yes, I believe he does."

I said, "Okay, I'll do it. Let's set it up tonight."

Michael and I met at Gameworks that night with some mutual friends, and boy, was I nervous. I'm talking underarms-sweating, hands-clammy kind of nervous.

I came dressed in what I thought would be appropriate for the occasion: wide-leg cargos, a fitted shirt, a hat, and some flat shoes. I thought we were going to talk and play games. That was not the case. In walks this tall, handsome man with the most gorgeous eyes I'd ever seen. As I watched him walk toward me, I took a short inventory of what he was working with: tall (check!), handsome (check!). He opened his mouth and greeted me by saying, "Woman of God" (double-check!), and last but not least, he was well-dressed (check!).

I mean this brotha came in suited up from top to bottom, gators and all. To be honest, I was kind of intimidated. I mean, what was I thinking in my cargos and T-shirt? (It was a very nice T-shirt, but a T-shirt nonetheless.) To make matters worse, I was so nervous that I cracked bad jokes to break the ice—which didn't work. He was focused like a laser beam, a man on a mission, seeking his future wife and mother of his children. That kind of focus is very sexy now, but I have to admit, back then it was very intimidating.

He asked me questions about likes and dislikes. Nothing too deep, because our friends were sitting there listening to every word. It turned out that he wasn't dressed up like that just for me but that he was on his way to a wedding reception for a friend. This dude had the audacity to ask me to go with him, and I looked at him like, "Yo, do you not see what I'm wearing? No, absolutely not. Not going. When I step out to something like that with you I need to be looking right, 'worthy' of the occasion. You go and we can meet up later."

This tall, confident, six-foot-six man said, "It's all good. You're with me." From that moment on, I knew he was my forever love. From the very beginning, he showed me the heart of Christ. I couldn't believe my ears. How could this man not care what clothes I had on? He was so secure, and he wanted me to rest in his security.

That was my first true encounter with Abba, and that encounter set me on a journey of discovering the "real" God: my Abba. Michael didn't care what I wore that night because he was honored to have me join him, and he was confident that me being with him and being me was enough. He was committed to holding me up, even in my insecurity.

Mature love is unselfish. It is a decision to love unconditionally, even when it's difficult.

That's the same way God feels about each one of His daughters. It's never been about who we are or what we have to offer. It's always been about His undying, unconditional love for us that says, "I could care less about what you look like, what you do for a living, how much money you have, or what great things you've accomplished. I just love you. I just want to be with you—the real you." Don't be afraid to show God who you really are. He thinks you're pretty terrific. After all, He made you. This conversation started to change the way I viewed myself. Was I immediately more secure? No, but there was a seed planted in my heart. The more I spent time meditating, praying, and talking with God, the more that seed began to grow. All that time was like water to that seed.

It takes a lot of work to rewire your brain to see the difference between mature and immature love. The patterns I saw made me a horrible friend and not the best romantic companion. I loved the idea of being in love but had no idea what it meant. Mature love is unselfish. It is a decision to love unconditionally, even when it's difficult. Before Michael, my relationships were over before they started. I would make up every excuse in my head why things wouldn't or couldn't work out. In most cases, the guys were knuckleheads, so that served me well. But when it was time to get married, not so much. Love and affection were the things I needed the most but liked least.

The idea of being vulnerable and letting someone see everything made me uncomfortable. What if they didn't like what they saw? Would they leave me? But that's just it: vulnerability is uncomfortable. It's allowing yourself the opportunity to experience freedom in relationships that's unmatched. This refusal to open up fully wasn't just reserved for nonfamilial relationships; I was also this way in the way I related to my parents and brothers. I robbed them of the opportunity to get to know me—the real me—because in my mind they had this image of who I was supposed to be, and who I really was didn't match that image. So I hid myself, because that sheltered me from the disappointment of disappointing others. The reality is that all this is about control—wanting to control how others see you—but the truth of who you are will always come to the surface, and eventually others will see. It would be bet-

ter to just relax and enjoy the process rather
than fighting against it.

Action Activity 8
Who have you distanced yourself from because you were scared they wouldn't like
the real you? Challenge yourself to call them
up and talk to them or invite them to dinner.
#GetRealJournalOp

Chapter 8

FINDING
YOUR TRIBE

She wears high heels. I wear sneakers.
She's cheer captain, and I'm on the bleachers.

—Taylor Swift

A s women, the relationships that we establish with other women are important to our development. By default, we focus on the people that make us feel good, but what's best for us may lie in the person that challenges us the most. We often shy away from the challenge because we don't have the proper foundation by which we can establish sisterhood in our lives. Most of us learn through trial and error, and the lessons come swift and with many battle scars. The problem with this method is that, as the lessons come, we have very little recovery time and have a tendency to make conclusions about relationships such as, "I just get along better with boys," or, "I don't know why females are so jealous of me." To go through life with these notions only limits you because the very place of frustration and pain has a beautiful possibility of transformation.

I'm challenging you to come face-to-face with yourself so that you may become a rescuer of your sister instead of her enemy.

I'm challenging you to come face-to-face with yourself so that you may become a rescuer of your sister instead of her enemy. Creating healthier relationships with other women definitely doesn't happen overnight. It takes work. I was that girl who didn't like girls very much, for many reasons. I felt intimidated when it seemed to me another female was "better" than me because I didn't see myself with the eyes of self-love and true identity. So I only really engaged in relationships with women who I felt I could help or mold. People weren't humans to me, they were projects—projects that I could complete to get affirmation that I was valuable and worthy.

Another reason I couldn't successfully engage in healthy friendships with other women was past experiences of being bullied because of my skin color and hair, being called ugly, and thinking I was fat. All the comments, the isolation, and the comparisons left me on the defensive when it came to my relationships with other women. I trusted very few because I had been a part of so many "friendships" gone sour. I've been in situations where I was betrayed and minimized when I tried to stick up for myself. When I was fairly young, I had a lot of friends that I found out were only my friends because my dad was the pastor. At times, I was pushed together with other kids because my parents were friends with their parents. There were instances where their parents had made comparisons between me and the other young ladies, and by the time we connected, the tension was quite evident and we found it difficult to move beyond our reputations.

In general, the women in my family on my maternal side are not very forgiving. They tend to hold grudges like none other in an effort to put the fear of God into anyone who might think of crossing them. Unfortunately, I inherited that trait. Before my spiritual awakening, I was not forgiving. I even held grudges against myself if I messed up. I loved being justified in my anger; however, it wreaked havoc on my relationships.

A poor foundation of friendships with other women left me timid, and I wasn't skilled at selecting friendships that were edifying. Instead, I chose friendships that cost me my peace, integrity, and joy. I was always on guard, and that gave way to comparison. How many of you have ever looked another girl up and down, as Taylor Swift did in her lyrics? Come on, admit it—checking out her shoes, outfit, and hair (and questioning whether it's all hers or not). Some of us have even compared the size of her body parts to ours. I've done it a bunch of times, all of which I explained to myself as "people watching."

People watching and comparing led me to so much internal agony. I was horrible to myself, so unkind and unforgiving. Does that resonate with any of you? The more I compared myself to other girls, the worse I felt and the lower my self-esteem sank. But no one could beat me up like I could. Most often, when we compare ourselves to others, we start off with how they are better than us in some way. Then we go on to think of all the ways we are better in an attempt to put ourselves on a pedestal. That's the part that makes us feel worse, because we start to be ashamed of our actions. It becomes a pattern. Rinse, repeat.

Too many times, I've let my constant need to compare myself to others control my emotions. This in turn affects my interactions with the ones I love. Case in point: when my husband has complimented me, I haven't even acknowledged it because I've been focused on my flaws. For most of us gals, it's hard to escape the temptation of comparing ourselves to others. The society we live in is media crazed and beauty obsessed. We can't help but to look on Pinterest, Facebook, Instagram, or any other social media outlet, for that matter, and think how much our lives suck, how bad a mom we are, how we have no style, how our hips are too big, how our butt is too small, and so on. The list can go on for days. These things are deceptions that get the self-critic going and are destructive to our well-being. If the deception succeeds, it will most definitely impact the next generation of women because it's almost impossible to impart purpose when you lack your own.

Don't get me wrong; I love Pinterest and Instagram. But if I'm not properly rooted and grounded in who God says I am as His daughter, I am in a world of trouble. Good things can come from observing others and the way they do things, but our identity can't be solely based on that. Comparisons should provoke you to be better, not tell you who you are. They should not weigh heavily on your mood.

Everyone wants to blame social media for our problem of comparing ourselves to others. The conversation always starts and stops there. But I think that social media is just the gasoline. The fire has already been burning within women. Social media has just perpetuated it. It starts out when we're little girls: Who is starting their period first? Who is thin? Who is thinner? Who is thinnest? I believe it has everything to do with being told from a young age that we have to be this way or that way in order to be accepted and liked not only by other females but by males too. Nothing robs us more of our true identity than the comparison of ourselves to another person.

We need to ask ourselves, where does the seed of self-comparison and not liking ourselves really start? Well, we can really point the finger to how we were parented. That conversation is important, but nobody wants to have it. For example, my husband Michael is a former professional athlete. He achieved an Olympic gold medal for the US and played on the NBA All-Star team. He even came back after two ACL injuries. That's pretty phenomenal. Our son, Michael II, is also very good at basketball, but he is also intellectually gifted. It's rare for a kid to have the athleticism gene as well as the gift of intellect.

His father and I have always said, "Whatever you want to do, son, we've got your back." Although we think that we're not pressuring him, sometimes the pressure is unspoken. Sometimes the pressure comes in a look, or in the silence, after your child comes to and says they want to quit an activity. Sometimes the pressure comes in the questions that the parent fires back at them. The truth is that our children are smarter and more intuitive than we think. And they know that we are not asking the questions to be curious. We are asking the questions because we are trying to actually persuade them a different way. I think that we are putting too much pressure on our kids to know what they have to do, what they want to do, and who they need to be. And it sends the unspoken message that they aren't enough just as they are. Our home lives, where we receive much of our reinforcement, start the fire, which is just made worse by social media. Many people believe they should take a "break" from it, and that's fine. Everybody across the board should take some time from social media now and then. However, more importantly, I think we should evaluate the reasons *why* we are on it, evaluate the reasons *why* we are posting, and develop the ability to discern whether a post or moment is just for us and our inner circle or if it's to share with everybody.

It's time to take a time-out from the toxicity of self-comparisons and the competition that arises from them. We need to live in an authentic place, be who God called us to be, and not worry about everyone else. We need to be real.

Nobody can beat you at being you. There's not another you on the planet, and God calls you His good work. I earnestly pray that all of you who are reading this and are brave enough to do the work to transform have a moment of spiritual awakening. From the awakening comes reformation, or what I like to call a restructuring of your mentality. This reformation will change the way you make choices about everything in your life. A few years

You should never try to fit in. You should belong.

ago, I was lonely and isolated, but now I'm in a place where I'm *choosing* solitude and am no longer lonely. Before, I didn't know myself, and I didn't know that I was an introvert. I thought that meant something negative. I was really busy trying to fit in and to be extroverted. You should never try to fit in. You should belong. *Fitting* is trying to change who you are to conform to your surroundings and expectations. But *belonging* is saying, "I am who I am, and that's the only person I can be." Regardless of what shape you are, you belong.

Not being lonely is not about having a lot of friends—it's about having the right friends. So how do you get the right friends? Well, you have to be honest about who you are. If you don't know who you are, you need to spend some time figuring that out. Take a real hard look in the mirror and be honest with yourself: What type of friend do you want? Have you been that type of friend?

Unfortunately, it often gets a lot worse before it gets better. Although you already may feel lonely, you'll need to take more time alone to truly get to know yourself. During my time of loneliness, I wasn't choosing solitude—solitude was choosing me. Answering the door when solitude knocks is a big deal, because the only way you're going to find out who you are is to spend time with yourself. Once you learn who you are, you'll know what kind of friends you need.

Another step to creating healthy relationships with women is learning to organize. Just as you organize your closet, you need to organize your relationships in life. Take inventory of your relationships: Is this a give-and-take relationship? Is this relationship filling your bucket? Is it pouring into you as much as you're pouring into it? How do you feel when you're with this person? Is this person too high-maintenance for you? Do you feel like you always have to make an effort?

In this way, you collect data for yourself.

Answering these questions allows you to identify your needs. During airplane safety presentations, flight attendants ask that, in the event of an emergency, you secure your own oxygen mask before helping others. Likewise, in life, you have to consider what your needs are first before you consider other people. Once you take that inventory, make a mental or written list of the things and relationships you have. Then, from your list, ask yourself what you're interested in keeping. Out of that list of dear friends you plan to keep, ask yourself if you've been a good friend to them. If you haven't been present and you haven't shown up for them, you need to apologize for that.

Throughout our lives, we try on relationships like we try on clothing. Sometimes older friendships, just like older items of clothing, get pushed to the side because you've got a newer, shinier item. But maybe it doesn't give you as much warmth and comfort as the older item once did. And then every time you find that older piece, you feel those warm fuzzies: "Oh my gosh, there it is." This situation happened in my relationship with an old friend. We didn't see each other a lot, and didn't talk to each other as much as we used to, but in taking inventory I realized how special her friendship was to me over twenty years. I realized I hadn't valued the relationship for years.

True freedom is contagious, so you are holding the keys to your freedom and the rescue of your sister. There is freedom in relationships and finding your tribe. Friendship is God's idea. He created us with the need to connect and belong. Part of the process of "letting go and letting God" is letting Him work through His people to bring healing to the areas that have been broken.

Chapter 9

PUTTING IT ALL TOGETHER

A trailblazer is a person who makes a new track through wild country or uncharted territory, a pioneer or innovator. I've been naturally inclined to live "outside the box" for quite some time—since birth, actually. But the fear of what others would think dictated a lot of my actions, and my people-pleasing, diplomatic nature played a part as well. Because I was the "good Christian girl," rebellion never seemed like an option. As I understood it, rebellion was questioning authority, thinking too many unconventional thoughts, and going against the "norm." So I conformed and temporarily forfeited my trailblazing nature.

Toxicity is a guaranteed way to delay your progress. Traumatic events and negative relationships breed unhealthy feelings, thoughts, and coping mechanisms. These are toxins that affect all aspects of our lives. We have to address toxicity and learn to be real with ourselves before we form relationships. We need to figure out who we truly are by being authentic, standing in our truth, realizing why we are the way we are, and recognizing if we hold toxicity from past experiences. Because even though you may be in a new relationship, you will continue toxic behaviors or patterns.

When we decide to confront the challenges of our lives, we are telling Abba that we trust Him to carry us through to the other side of an obstacle. That, my friends, is what being a trailblazer is all about. And that is true and total freedom. Let's explore a little further.

Well-behaved women seldom make history.
—Laurel Thatcher Ulrich

So what does living out loud look like? Do we have to dress according to trend and be ten pounds underweight? Do we have to use social media as our measuring stick for success? Can we as women actually attain the freedom of not having to be liked by everyone?

The good news is this: You have no responsibility to be anything but who God made you to be. You have the freedom to do only what the Divine Father says to do—no more, no less. It is in our best interest to silence the other voices that have tried to mislabel us with expectations that aren't ours to carry.

I have to admit, it's not easy to hold true

to your authenticity. As I mentioned, I was tested in this area of my relationships with a few people. I had an expectation of how I wanted to be treated, and that expectation didn't line up with their behavior. One of the biggest mistakes you can make in a relationship is holding other people to your set of beliefs. You will be disappointed every time. I was hurt and angry because I felt rejected and let down. I was faced with a choice right then and there: Was I going to revert to their set of beliefs and behaviors and compromise my authenticity, or was I going to remain true to who I was? For about two days I pondered this question, and I ultimately chose to stand firm in my beliefs and how I think people should be treated. I know it temporarily feels good to get revenge and do to others what they do to us, but that never lasts. It's not worth it.

What does holding true to authenticity look like in real life? When someone doesn't speak, you speak. When someone doesn't acknowledge when something important happens in your life—for example, a birthday—you be sure to acknowledge theirs. Never base your actions on how another behaves. Be true to yourself, stand firm in your beliefs, and treat people how you'd like to be treated, not how they treat you. For many, "being real" gives them an excuse to be mean. These people go around being rude to people under the pretense of not being fake and "keeping it real." Trust me, I've heard this time and time again. This exchange happens, especially between women. Let me paint this picture for you:

You're invited to a party and you've heard through the grapevine that another woman you don't necessarily vibe with is going to be there. You decide to go to the party anyway with the intention of not making an issue out of it. There will be other people there that you get along with. You go to the party and you catch the gaze of this other female's side-eye toward you. Despite the apparent shade, you press on, smile, and say hi, but inside you are madder than a hornet. I mean, the audacity of the side-eye, right?

Sound familiar to anyone? This has happened to me several times. So many times, in fact, that it almost seems like a rite of passage as a member of my gender. Simply put, if it hasn't happened to you and you are a female, keep living! You can dislike a person or not get a person and still speak to them. It's called being polite—better yet, it's called being a grown-up. Let's not mistake "being real" for being immature.

A truly authentic life is not based on the behaviors or actions of others. It's based on your standards and the principles you set for yourself. In this scenario, one would assume that this negative exchange was either warranted in some way or that the "bully" was just being mean. I wish it were that simple. Many people use the phrase "keeping it real" as a badge of honor to hide the fact that they really are hiding themselves. Isn't that ironic? Truth is, many of us are not outgoing because of the fear of rejection, or we dislike ourselves so much that we don't believe that anyone else would like us either.

Nothing will impede our connections with other women more quickly than the feelings of unworthiness and self-hatred. Although this may sound like common sense, it's also a common problem within the female community. It's very difficult to present yourself authentically when you don't like, love, or value yourself or when you don't feel worthy of love because you're ashamed of who you are. The justification for not reaching out to connect becomes all too commonplace. We will find ourselves facing the mirror with our eyes tightly shut, telling ourselves that we are too ugly and broken to look at. This practice will either give way to complete avoidance of developing new relationships or the avoidance of getting to know oneself's true identity.

Another common excuse I hear often is, "I'm an introvert." I hate to break it to you, but introverts are not necessarily mean-spirited and shy because they fear rejection. Being an introvert doesn't mean not being outgoing. I'm a textbook introvert, but no one would ever know. I love people and I love to talk to people. For the introvert, that's never the issue. It's more about how you hold onto, give out, and receive energy. I used to think that time was the most valuable thing, but I've come to see that my energy is even more important than my time. So while I used to attempt to use my introversion as an excuse to not build relationships with people, I came to realize that it went much deeper than that. Living your truth out loud will be the bravest thing you do. Dig deep and give others the gift of yourself. Don't let fear inhibit you. Instead, let it motivate you from the inside out.

Action Activity 9

What are some of the dreams you had as a child? Go back to those and fantasize. What emotions come up? Do you still want to pursue those dreams? Think about how your dreams have changed. What do you want to do now? What are you most passionate about? #GetRealJournalOp

---

Chapter 10

PAYING IT FORWARD

Paying it forward is a lot like being a trail-blazer. You can't go forward unless you take a look backward. For example, when you have a dream or a goal you'd like to achieve, it's easy to feel like you're alone in that pursuit. But you're not. In fact, there are many others in history who have done the things you're looking to do, just during a different time period.

It does us justice to look at women throughout history who have made a difference. True, we won't be able to learn everything from one single person or situation, but taking a look backward gives us an idea of how things might go in the future. We should glean not only from past successes but past mistakes as well. These help transition us into trailblazers, so that we may be prepared for our particular assignment, whatever that may be.

All throughout history, we read stories of women who have made a difference in "their" world. I put quotations around the word *their* because, before they had a global impact, these individuals worked within their sphere of influence. When it became clear to me that part of my life's work was to help inspire women to be an inspiration, I heightened my study of women across the generations that came before me. As I pursue what's ahead, I'm always thinking of both the ones who have come before and those who will come after me. Let's explore some of my personal favorite trailblazing women that I came across in my studies.

QUEEN ESTHER

Queen Esther, also known as Hadassah, was a Jewish orphan. She was extremely beautiful, and her uncle knew she was somehow going to make things better for her captive people. When the king of Persia sought a new wife, Esther, who was keeping her Jewish identity a secret, blew him away with her beauty and humility. Fortunately, that's all it took for the king to be smitten by her. Later, when the regent Haman convinced the king to pass a law ordering the death of all Jews, Esther appeared before the king to plead for her people despite her fear of losing her life. The rest is history. Because she had humility and let her inner beauty shine through, she was able to save the Jews from slaughter. Every time she appeared before the king, she risked her life. Her attitude was, "If I am to die, let me die." Her only concern was for others.

HARRIET TUBMAN

Harriet Tubman was born into slavery in Maryland in 1820. Twenty-nine years later, in 1849, she escaped to the North and became the most famous "conductor" of the

Underground Railroad. Tubman risked her life to lead hundreds of slaves from the plantation system to freedom on this elaborate secret network of safe houses. Tubman was a prominent member of the abolitionist movement before the Civil War, and she also worked as a spy for the Union. After the war, Tubman dedicated her life to helping the poor.

Harriet Tubman, in my opinion, had the same fearless mentality as Queen Esther. She was a Moses to her people because she was going to lead them out of captivity into freedom. That fearless, no-nonsense attitude of, "Whatever it takes, whatever needs to be done, I'm going to do it," is something that we can all learn from.

HELEN KELLER

We all have heard stories of Helen Keller, the blind and deaf author, educator, and activist. While studying her life, I was so overcome with pride as a fellow woman. She was able to overcome her adversity to become one of the twentieth century's leading humanitarians.

Helen Adams Keller was born on June 27, 1880, in Tuscumbia, Alabama. Two years later, she contracted an illness that took her sight and hearing. Her teacher, Anne Sullivan, helped Keller learn to communicate, and Keller was able to graduate college at age twenty-four, becoming the first deaf-blind person to achieve a bachelor's degree. She went on to write twelve books, give many lectures, and cofound the ACLU.

For her whole life, Keller focused on how she could improve the lives of others. In particular, she passionately pursued women's rights and equality for people with disabilities. She could have easily given up, and I don't think anyone would have blamed her. But for Keller, giving up was simply not an option. How many of us can say the same?

Despite all of her challenges, Helen Keller was relentless in the face of adversity. She is undoubtedly the epitome of the Real Girls FART acronym.

MALALA YOUSAFZAI

Malala Yousafzai is one of the more current world-changers I've studied. The Taliban controlled her country and did not want girls to have rights to anything, much less an education. At the age of fourteen, Malala was shot in the head because she refused to remain silent regarding the injustices in her country. When she got an opportunity to share her story with the world, she insisted to her father that, despite the dangers, she had to do it. "When the whole world is silent," she said, "even one voice becomes powerful." She went on to be the youngest person to ever win the Nobel Peace Prize.

> *Not everybody has the same color, the*
> *same language, or the same customs, but*
> *they have the same heart, the same blood,*
> *and the same need for love.*

—Josephine Baker

What these women all have in common are their fearlessness and determination. Each of them had tragedy, baggage, and stuff that made them seem undesirable in some way. They pushed past all that and went on to accomplish great feats. We are all called on some level to facilitate change in our sphere of influence.

I already know what some of you are thinking: *These women are all great, but they are special. They've got that special something that I don't have. I could never be as brave as any of these women.* That couldn't be further from the truth. The fact that you chose to read this book to change your life took courage. Something deep inside your gut knew when you read the title that you needed to attain freedom. To get to a free place you have to first acknowledge and face those ugly places, those undesirable things.

The comparison game that we play with ourselves is lethal to our God-given potential because it allows us to think that we aren't enough, that we need to be more like this or that to be brave or make a difference. But the fact is that you are enough, more than enough, to have influence. We have to let go of who we think we should be and embrace what is.

We have to let go of who we think we should be and embrace what is.

Although we may be different from our sisters, the one thing that unites us all is the desire to belong and give ourselves to something bigger than us.

This alone is what inspired my blog, *Real Girls F.A.R.T.* It has been a divine, ongoing undoing of all my preconceived ideas of what and who I should be. When I went through my breakdown, a.k.a. my spiritual awakening, I knew inside that there was a deeper purpose for my suffering and that I wasn't the only woman dealing with these things. My suffering gave birth to the real me and lit a fire within me that couldn't be contained. Sometimes, we want to escape our pain, but it's necessary to feel the ache to alert us that there's a bigger issue we need to address. Our Divine Father never wastes an experience. I am convinced that everything that I've gone through and will continue to walk through will be used at some point to help someone else. If my pain does nothing else but awaken my empathy and compassion, then it's done enough.

I encourage you to get comfortable with being uncomfortable. Share your story proudly and loudly. Wear your scars as a badge of honor and know that what didn't kill you woke you up. Community is a large part of healing, and if you fail to let others help you, you are hindering them in their call to pay it forward. Embrace your pain, and know that in order to feel pain you must be alive. Welcome to the rocket ship of self-discovery. You will be amazed at what you accomplish.

We all have a sphere of influence, but you can only use it when you know who you are and when you begin to see yourself the way God sees you. You are a living, breathing solution to the world's problems. You are not an afterthought. God loves women, and He created us all in His image. You don't have to change your shape to fit. You already belong and are where you are supposed to be at this moment. So rise up, woman. Disrupt the universe by changing "your" world. You are enough now and always have been.

Action Activity 10

Start a study on different women in history who braved the wild to make a difference in their world. Note the personal tragedies that motivated them, and how they overcame those obstacles. During your study, keep a journal of your findings. *#GetRealJournalOp*

IN EARLY 2016, Achea Redd was diagnosed with Generalized Anxiety Disorder. After hiding her condition out of fear and shame, Achea quickly realized it was only getting worse, affecting her physically to the point of a nervous breakdown. It wasn't until she acknowledged the situation with her loved ones, seeking out treatment from her therapist and doctor, that things started to get better.

As a form of self-expression and healing, Achea created her own blog, sharing her feelings about mental health and authenticity. The flow of support she received from the community compelled her to create Real Girls F.A.R.T.—a space to empower and equip women with the necessary tools to use their voices and become their best, most authentic selves. Achea currently resides in Columbus, Ohio with her husband, Michael, and her two children.